GREEN
HOUSE

GREEN HOUSE

NORM CRAMPTON

*eco-friendly
disposal and
recycling at home*

M. EVANS
Lanham • New York • Boulder • Toronto • Plymouth, UK

Published by M. Evans
An imprint of The Rowman & Littlefield Publishing Group, Inc.
4501 Forbes Boulevard, Suite 200, Lanham, Maryland 20706
www.rlpgtrade.com

Estover Road | Plymouth PL6 7PY | United Kingdom

Distributed by NATIONAL BOOK NETWORK

Library of Congress Cataloging-in-Publication Data

Crampton, Norman.
  Green house : eco-friendly disposal and recycling at home / Norm Crampton.
     p. cm.
  ISBN-13: 978-1-59077-139-6 (pbk. : alk. paper)
  ISBN-10: 1-59077-139-7 (pbk. : alk. paper)
  1. Recycling (Waste, etc.)—Citizen participation. 2. Waste minimization—Citizen participation.
3. Salvage (Waste, etc.)—Citizen participation. 4. Refuse and refuse disposal—Environmental
aspects. 5. Environmental protection—Citizen participation. 6. Home economics. I. Title.
  TD171.7C73 2008
  640—dc22   2007051484

Printed on recycled paper.

♾ The paper used in this publication meets the minimum requirements of American National Standard for Information Sciences—Permanence of Paper for Printed Library Materials, ANSI/NISO Z39.48-1992.

Manufactured in the United States of America.

CONTENTS

CONTENTS

CONTENTS

ACKNOWLEDGMENTS

Thanks to Dan Gajus and Greg Rood, Hoosier Disposal; to Ralph Gray, Professor of Economics, DePauw University; to Scott Morgan, Monroe County Solid Waste Management District; to Steven Boggs, Indiana Department of Environmental Management; to Jane St. John, longtime colleague in recycling, friend, and adviser; and especially to Frederick Macaulay Crampton, my son, who sensed it was the right time to revise *Complete Trash,* the first edition of this book.

INTRODUCTION: UNSTUFFING

This is a no-fault guide to living a greener life. No wagging fingers or tut-tuts here. God knows you're doing the patriotic thing, bringing home all the goodies and renting storage for the surplus. And you're decisive—you know when it's time to toss the old stuff, and you have no qualms.

And yet—the climate is warming and the icebergs are melting. Maybe it's time to change habits. Notice I don't say *your* habits—could be your neighbor's habits. You've got your eye on him. You watch what she's putting out on garbage day. It makes you sick to see him send perfectly good stuff to the landfill or incinerator. That's not *your* style. You believe in the Three R's—Reduce, Reuse, Recycle—most of the time.

Anyway, what's the rush? What does trash have to do with global warming? Doesn't Big G Green mean biking to work, buying a hybrid car, burning less coal?

What does that have to do with taking out the garbage?

I'm glad you asked, because there really is a connection between trash and global warming. The link is more subtle than watching glaciers shrink in Greenland, but it's just as real.

One problem is at the front end, where trash is born innocently as wonderful manufactured stuff—suave, stylish, enticing items that speed us on the pursuit of happiness, plus more ordinary items from the paper aisle at the supermarket. But whimsical or essential, everything produced for the marketplace requires energy, especially electric power and motor fuel, the two big producers of the global-warming carbon dioxide.

It's pretty simple—more stuff equals more greenhouse gas. Sure, you could manufacture off the grid. You could get your power from an old windmill and walk your products to the bazaar. But that's no way to fund a 401(k).

At the other of the trash cycle, you're amazed to see all that stuff pile up in your neighbor's garbage bin—bags, boxes, jugs, bottles, cans, barbeque, old newspapers, batteries, carpet, junk mail, light bulbs, phone books, day-old deli, coffee grounds, diapers, soggy pizza, orange peels, eggshells, inkjet cartridges, kitty litter, past-date drugs, old TVs, old clothes, old cell phones, old old old.

Viewing this mess, deep in your gut you feel another big shot of global warming gas is just down the block and around the corner, where an incinerator burns the trash, producing more carbon dioxide; or where a landfill swallows the trash, digests some of it, and burps methane, an even more potent global warmer.

So trash is a warming agent both when it's pristine new stuff and sullied old stuff. This book doesn't dwell on the front end, where you decide what to buy—that's between you, your wallet, and your higher nature. But this book does talk about your choices at the back end for disposing of stuff in the best way, the green way, to reduce the impact your trash has on climate change. Think of this book as a user's guide to the garbage can.

For the record, this book has a bias against burning trash but not against burying it. Garbage dumps are as old as civilization, and they keep archeologists busy. Often there's no alternative to burying old stuff. But this book urges the better, energy-saving alternatives—recy-cling, reusing, reducing.

Finally, one all-purpose disclaimer. The views and recommendations expressed here are my own, based on experience and the most recent technical information. In all cases, the last word on every trash question belongs to your local waste-management professionals. This is a friendly way of saying that neither the author nor the publisher is liable for any injury, humiliation, or public scorn you may suffer as a result of following the advice in *Green House*. We'll take full credit, however, for the personal satisfaction you gain in getting rid of your stuff in a greener way.

Norm Crampton
Bloomington, Indiana

ALUMINUM CANS

Aluminum beverage cans are worth at least 2 cents each at the local scrap dealer. That may not seem much, but curbside recycling programs depend on aluminum cans to help cover costs—they're the only household discard that pays its own way around the recovery-reuse cycle. So next time you buy a 24-can case of drinks, imagine about 50 cents in recycling value. If you contribute the empties to your city collection program, the yield is even higher because of volume.

If those numbers fail to excite interest, consider that the typical empty aluminum can is remelted, remade, refilled, and back on the store shelf within 60 days. That's practically metaphysical. The green advantage is even more compelling—aluminum made from recycled cans requires only 5% of the electric power that it takes to convert virgin bauxite ore into aluminum. Less power equals less carbon dioxide into the atmosphere. All of which makes you wonder why Americans aren't doing a better job of recycling aluminum cans. The recovery rate has been virtually stagnant at a little over 50% for the past 20 years.

Green way to get rid of aluminum cans: Recycle all of them, and let virtue be your reward.

AMMONIA-BASED CLEANERS

Hmmm—so you have some common household cleaners to dispose of. Maybe you've run out of elbow grease. Ah, but that's enough examination of motives. The answer, please!

Green way to get rid of ammonia and ammonia-based cleaners: If you absolutely cannot use the leftovers for window washing, floor scrubbing, etc., pour the remains down the sink with plenty of water, or down the toilet; rinse the container, and toss the bottle into the recycling bin.

WARNING: Never mix ammonia with chlorine bleach. Some people have done this thinking they would get a more powerful cleaning agent. Instead, they get a deadly gas and, ironically, a liquid that has virtually no cleaning power compared to the separate chemicals.

Folks who like to change the car antifreeze by them- selves are an endangered species, and that's a good thing. Possibly because antifreeze is a hazardous waste; possibly because virtually all new and newer cars and pickups use extended-life engine coolants, with recom- mended change intervals of five years or 100,000 miles, most worn-out antifreeze drains into drums at auto re- pair shops for periodic collection by commercial recy- cling businesses. But if you're still doing this work in the home garage, take note:

ANTIFREEZE

Green way to dispose of old antifreeze: Save it in a metal can or plastic bottle until you take the vehicle in for other service. Then pass the old antifreeze to your mechanic for recycling. Don't flush antifreeze down the toilet; don't pour it into a storm sewer. And never, ever pour antifreeze on the ground. It has a sweet taste that's attractive to pets, and it's lethal.

APPLIANCES

Large

If you want to sound like an expert, speak of large household appliances the way professionals do. Call them "white goods," so-named because most stoves, refrigerators, freezers, washing machines, dryers, microwave ovens, and water heaters used to be white. Even if they're another color, they're still "white goods" to the trade—and a recycling success story. At least 85% of large household appliances go direct to the scrap yard for recovery of steel bodies, iron parts, copper innards, switches, refrigerant gas, compressor oil, etc. Steel is by far the largest item recovered, averaging 123 pounds in a refrigerator, according to the industry. Most states ban disposal of white goods, but even when white goods do arrive at the landfill, they're usually pulled aside for recycling.

Green way to get rid of large appliances: If you're buying new, hauling away the old unit is almost always part of the deal with the store. If not, negotiate to include this service; and be prepared to pay a little, if necessary. Or store the old unit in your garage until the community has a bulk items pick-up day.

Special note about refrigerators and freezers: It's against the law in most places to discard them without first removing the door or lid or any kind of lock that prevents opening from the inside. This is to avoid creating a deadly trap for kids at play.

You're kidding, repair a small household appliance? Thanks to the global economy, it's much cheaper to toss small appliances and buy new. Things like clock radios, toasters, and old TVs simply can't be put back in service without spending far more than they are worth—assuming you can find repair service at all. (See more on TVs at the listing "E-waste.") Fixing little electrical things used to be a decent occupation. But so was door-to-door sales.

APPLIANCES
Small

Green way to get rid of small appliances: None. Tossing that old toaster or clock radio into the trash may not be the best use of resources but you probably have no choice.

ASHES

Fireplace Ashes

Wood ashes are rich in potassium. Flowers and vegetables need potassium to grow well and resist disease. The connection is obvious. "But don't overdo it," a horticulturist advises. "Sometimes people get carried away," spreading ashes so heavily that the balance with other nutrients is upset. A Penn State expert cautions to keep wood ashes under 20 pounds per thousand square feet of garden.

Green way to get rid of wood ashes: Spread a judicious amount in the garden. Throw the rest in the trash: Wood ashes from a home fireplace are unlikely to do harm in a landfill.

Human Remains

Human ashes—"cremains," as they're called in the undertaking business—can be disposed of in many ways other than the familiar encryptment in church or cemetery. Officially speaking, disposition of a human body is considered final in the crematory. What happens to the ashes is up to the survivors. Just keep it "dignified," says one undertaker. Dignity does not include scattering ashes on any body of fresh water, however. That is considered pollution. Ocean disposal is less restrictive. A

Boston mortician recalls chartering a fishing vessel to take the survivors and the dear departed out for a scattering in the Atlantic.

Certain military veterans are eligible for a more elaborate ceremony at sea. Upon notification from a military Office of Decedent Affairs, the Navy will assign a ship to take a canister of human ashes to sea and dispatch it to the ocean bottom. The next of kin receive a flag and a report of the exact latitude and longitude where the remains were tossed over.

If that's too dramatic a finale, your backyard is a fine place to spread ashes or bury a canister. Or you can put old Uncle Normie on the mantel, but please don't use a clear glass container. I will not be looking my best.

Check with local authorities before disposing of cremains on public lands.

BATTERIES

Car Batteries

Car batteries used to be a terrible problem and, ironically, the Environmental Protection Agency was at least partly to blame. In its zeal to protect the environment, the EPA enacted tough rules about who pays for the cleanup if dumped wastes poisoned underground water supplies. Under the law, even a well-meaning battery recycler who followed the rules could be found liable for the neglect of some less-responsible company further around the recycling loop. Many battery recyclers quit the business. Recycling rates for car batteries dropped to as low as 60%. Most of the remaining 40% were dumped in landfills, releasing millions of pounds of lead and millions of gallons of sulfuric acid into the environment. So much for good intentions.

Then the states got smart, prohibiting dumping of lead-acid batteries, enacting front-end deposit laws, and attracting recyclers back into business. Today, most places that sell car batteries also take them back. There's a lot of good stuff in a dead battery—about 21 pounds of lead, three pounds of plastic, and a gallon of sulfuric acid. All can be processed for reuse. Today, at least 95% of car batteries are recycled.

Green way to get rid of a car battery: Return it to the dealer when you buy new, even if you have to pay a small recycling fee. Some scrap metals dealers buy old car batteries—check the classified directory under "Recycling Centers."

If you have a choice, choose a rechargeable battery over a single-use battery. If a product label doesn't specify a particular battery type, you can generally use a rechargeable. Yes, they cost more up front, but over the lifetime of the battery or the device it's powering, rechargeables cost less; and the end-of-life routine probably will be recycling or recovery and reuse of the battery's contents. That's much better than tossing a one-use alkaline cell in the garbage can (see the entry below, "A, C, D, 9-Volt, and Button Batteries").

BATTERIES

Laptop, Cell Phone, and Other Rechargeable Batteries

Green way to get rid of a rechargeable battery: Take it back to where you bought it. Most retailers will take these batteries back for free—certainly when you're buying a replacement. California and New York City are leading the way in consumer convenience. They require retailers to take back without charge all the brands of rechargeable batteries that they sell. If you don't live in California or New York City, you can find the nearest drop-off site by calling 1-877-2-Recycle or 1-800-8Battery and entering your zip code. Or go online at www.rbrc.org/call2recycle.

For details on the California and New York City

battery take-back laws, plus a comparison of European Union and U.S. regulations, take a look at this website: www.informinc.org/candore.pdf. To find where you can donate or recycle electronic items containing rechargeable batteries, check the EPA site, which provides links to major manufacturers and retailers: www.epa.gov/epaoswer/hazwaste/recycle/ecycling/donate.htm.

BATTERIES

A, C, D, 9-Volt, and Button Batteries

As all kids know, Santa Claus maintains a huge warehouse of AA, AAA, C, and D batteries. An estimated 40% of all battery sales occur during the weeks before Christmas, and a very large proportion hit the trash, dead, by early January.

The small, single-use batteries that power flashlights, radios, clocks, toys, and smoke detectors are okay for landfill burial. That was not always the case. Before the contemporary alkaline battery, these common small batteries contained mercury, a toxin. But the mercury has been gone for about 10 years.

Button batteries are different. The small, silver batteries used in hearing aids and watches do contain mercury (it's used to help maintain battery voltage) and must be treated as hazardous waste.

Green way to get rid of small, household batteries: Button batteries must be handed over for household hazardous waste processing to recover the mercury. Hearing aid sellers and watch dealers usually collect them. But nonrechargeable AA, AAA, C, D, and 9-volt batteries can go in the trash for landfill disposal.

Note: If your trash goes to an incinerator, take care to drop your batteries in a collection box—burning an alkaline battery releases harmful gases to the atmosphere. If you don't know whether the trash is buried or burned, assume it's burned. The obvious better behavior is to quit buying one-life batteries and switch to rechargeables.

You already know how a bicycle can change a life. Remember when you first learned to ride? Remember the pure delight of your offspring when they soloed on a

BICYCLES

two-wheeler? Bikes can make wonderful things happen. That's especially true for people who cannot afford a bike.

Green way to get rid of a bicycle in working condition: Donate it to one of the nonprofit organizations that collects bikes for reuse by other folks at home and abroad. Try one of those listed below.

If delivery of your bike to a collection site is a problem, get creative: Create a bicycle cooperative in your community. Any of the listed groups can advise, and you might take a look at Cyclo North-South (www.cyclonordsud.org), the Montreal group that wrote the book on this splendid way to turn old wheels into new hope.

Or you may be able to ship your bike to the nearest site:

- Bikes Across Borders, Austin, Texas: www.bikesacrossborders.org
- Bikes Not Bombs, Boston, Massachusetts: www.bikesnotbombs.org
- Working Bikes Cooperative, Chicago, Illinois: www.workingbikes.org

- Pedals for Progress, High Bridge, New Jersey:
  www.p4p.org
- Bicycles for Humanity, Kelowna, British
  Columbia: www.bicycles-for-humanity.org
- Bikes for the World, Washington, DC:
  www.bikesfortheworld.org

BIRD-CAGE LINER

The stuff that falls on bird-cage liner is rich in nitrogen and phosphorus and makes good fertilizer for indoor plants. Deep doodoo will nourish an indoor forest. You may gain some satisfaction, if not absorbency, by lining the cage with credit card statements and past-due notices, for example. Thus, as the guano deepens you are both protecting the cage and adding insult to injury.

Green way to get rid of bird-cage liner: If you use newspaper, composting is a fine idea. Otherwise, into the trash bin.

BOOKS

So you're moving across town or across country and decide to empty the bookshelves—reduce dead weight, ease back strain. Deciding what to pack and what to dump is the time for honesty and hindsight. Honestly, you're never going to read Sir Winston Churchill's six-volume set on World War II, despite the elegant binding. And hindsight suggests you don't need *Why the Real Estate Boom Won't Go Bust*, at least for a while. After careful consideration you have a stack of perfectly good books, some in mint condition, seeking a new home.

Green way to get rid of books: Contribute them to a book sale for a good cause. Fair weather is the likeliest time for these events, though the sponsors may be stockpiling well beforehand. Libraries and schools raise funds by selling old books at garage-sale prices. Call your local public library to find out what's happening.

Most books in home libraries have only rummage-sale value, a librarian advises. So don't expect any money for them. Old textbooks generally have zero value, and encyclopedias are "dangerous" to pass along, the librarian warns. In a world of Wikipedia, dipping into a vintage Britannica is as risky as eating old chicken salad.

Second best green way to get rid of books: Burn them, especially apt for that dog-eared copy of Fahrenheit 451. Because the bindings on some books clog paper-salvaging machinery, hardcovers especially but paperbacks, too, are of little interest to paper recycling programs. So let those old plots catch fire one last time in the fireplace.

BOOZE

For some reason you have to dispose of stale beer, bad wine, and open bottles of spirits. Pouring them down the drain with plenty of water is perfectly okay. But are there more creative solutions? Certainly. For example, some people say beer makes a good shampoo rinse; you can make room for a few bottles in the shower. Also, a semi-dry wine—10% to 11% alcohol—left open for several weeks will become a nice vinegar, experts say. And a half-empty bottle of booze, dressed up with a nice ribbon, may be a jolly gift to a neighbor who dabbles in spirits.

Green way to get rid of booze: Dispose of the contents (see above), rinse the container, and recycle. Be sure the bottles are empty. Partially-filled bottles create a greater hazard of flying glass if they are crushed in a collection truck.

BULLETS

Bullets and shotgun shells are considered hazardous waste, no surprise. Mildly surprising is the apparent number of bullets and shells casually residing with cuff-link collections or in kitchen drawers. The desk sergeant at a local police station says bullets are turned in "with some frequency," and this is not the Wild West.

Green way to get rid of bullets: Take them to the nearest police station. And be prepared to identify yourself—a report will be made.

CAMERAS

Digital cameras pushed film cameras into the closet quicker than you can say eBay. While the Internet marketplace may produce a little cash for your old Canon, Minolta, or Nikon, I like the suggestion of a guy in Britain. He says, display your historic film camera alongside a favorite photograph you made with that camera.

A small tripod will make a good mount for the camera. Or reuse that heavy old single-lens-reflex as a bookend.

Disposing of a digital camera should pose no problem. If you don't want to deal with an eBay auction, give it to a school for classroom use, or drop it off at Goodwill and declare a tax deduction for current market value.

CARPET

That roll of dirty old carpet may seem totally worthless. In fact, a considerable business now exists to turn worn-out carpet into useful new products, like plastic car parts, plastic lumber—even drainage tiles. The problem is, what do you do right now with this heavy hunk of stuff?

Green way to get rid of carpet: If the carpet is not dirty and worn but like new—you're pulling it for new décor—call the local Habitat for Humanity. If you can provide a large amount of carpet, say, 800 square feet, there may be a good new home for it. Otherwise, Habitat may be interested in your good condition carpet for resale. But if the old carpet has many tales to tell, first, ask your new-carpet installer what plans he has for recycling. If none, press on: Ask your retailer to research ways to keep old carpet out of the landfill—you may encounter a teaching opportunity. You may wish to pass along the phone number of an Indianapolis company that does nothing but recycle carpet: Kruse Carpet Recycling, 317-337-1950. Or get in touch with the company yourself: www.krusecarpetrecycling.com.

CARS

In the greenest of all green worlds, hardly anyone would have to personally get rid of a car because hardly anyone would own a car. Most cars would be owned by commercial fleets like Zipcar, Flexcar, or Boulder, Colorado's CarShare, providing a car for short-term use, day or night. Public transportation would be so available and so good that you'd hardly need a car, anyway. Taxis would be clean, cheap, safe, fast, and heavily subsidized by a hefty new federal gasoline tax. Taxi drivers would happily wait at the supermarket or laundry while you ran errands—almost like having your own chauffeur.

Granted, living comfortably without a car does

sound like a fantasy. But some of the essentials already are in place in urban areas. CarSharing.net counts upwards of 50 urban locations all across the nation where you can join a car-sharing program and rent a car by the hour or the day. (To find a location, see the web listing below.) The same kind of service is available on some college campuses—take a look at Zipcar.com for some locations and program details. Rental car companies are adding hybrids to their fleets. Mass transit is very good in a handful of places, pretty good in many places, but pretty awful in others. And taxis as a rule are available when you don't need them.

So, patience is in order. But just think of the dividends from going car-less: No hunting for a parking place, no car insurance, no monthly car payments ever, no pricey repairs or ridiculous gasoline prices. More money into your 401(k)!

Green way to get rid of a car: If it's really a piece of junk, turn it over to a scrap metal dealer. Look in the classified directory under "Scrap Metal Processing and Recycling." If the car is serviceable, consider donating it to a charitable organization for resale or reuse. You've heard about these charitable appeals for years: Do good by donating your car; do well by getting a tax deduction in return.

If donating the car sounds appealing, take care to (1) make the donation directly to a tax-exempt organization—a 501(c)(3) organization—not to a third-party broker; and (2) make sure the title is transferred to the tax-exempt organization by name, and keep a copy. You can search for tax-qualified organizations by name at the IRS website below (click on the link "Search for Exempt Organizations"). The same site tells you about additional paperwork if you're claiming a deduction.

In general, you can deduct no more than the fair market value of the car in its current condition. Good operating condition is important. Tom and Ray, the "Tappet Brothers" of Car Talk on National Public Radio, say a donated car should be no more than 10 years old and in use sometime within the two months prior to donation. They offer further counsel at www.cartalk.com/content/features/vehicledonation/. To verify that an organization is tax-exempt, check www.irs.gov/charities/article/0,,id=139024,00.html. To

find a car-sharing company, go to www.carsharing
.net/where.html.

P.S. Whatever you decide to do about the car, remember the words of William Clay Ford Jr., the
great-grandson of Henry, speaking a few years ago:
"The day will come when car ownership becomes
antiquated. If you live in a city, you don't need a
car." (That rattling sound is his great-grandfather
turning over in his grave.)

CAR WAX

Car wax and chrome polish contain petroleum distillates—hazardous wastes. If you throw a half-empty can
into the trash there's an 80% chance it will go to a
landfill, where the toxics can be drawn into underground water supplies.

Green way to get rid of car wax: Give away the un-
used portion to a car buff—an auto detailer will be
grateful for free supplies. Kids in a high school auto
class may be interested. Otherwise, save it for the
next neighborhood hazardous-wastes cleanup day.

CAT LITTER

As a dog lover, I write this with a sense of superiority. Cats get the white-glove treatment with their discreet little litter boxes behind frilly curtains. Dogs do it outside, where the stuff belongs, back on good old terra firma, at least until you scoop the poop.

People who study these things say the frequency of changing cat litter depends mostly on the cat lover's nose, and that cats have a higher tolerance for dirty litter boxes than owners do. The volume of cat litter is staggering. According to a national survey of pet owners, cats outnumber dogs 90 million to 73 million. If your weekly dump of cat litter is 4 pounds, the weekly national total is 180,000 tons; annually, 9.36 million tons, or just about the weight of Uranus.

Green way to get rid of cat litter: Into the trash can. But whenever possible, try to get double duty from the litter by using it to soak up other difficult disposables such as oily, fatty stuff—kitchen grease, for example. The litter will absorb it and help to prevent pollution of groundwater near landfills.

Green way to get rid of CDs and DVDs: Try everything to avoid trashing them. Discs in playable condition containing commercial entertainment are great items at neighborhood fund-raisers or as giveaways to friends. Recycling and recovery of the polycarbonate body for other uses is possible, although not through most community recycling programs. Call local officials to find out. CDs and DVDs containing personal information must, of course, be rendered unplayable before disposal. Buy a shredder? Maybe you know someone with a shredder to borrow. But, really, considering the hundreds of times you can erase and rewrite to a CD or DVD in a burner, there's little excuse for ever tossing one.

A note on the bottom of my Raisin Bran box says the carton is "Made from 100% recycled paperboard—Minimum 35% post-consumer content." That means that about one-third of the paper fiber in the box comes from cartons recycled by households, and about two-thirds comes from clean scrap paper—trimmings, mainly—collected at carton manufacturing plants. Those proportions are pretty much true for all food cartons. Manufacturers understood the importance of recovering scrap long before the rest of us did.

Green way to get rid of food cartons: If your town requires you to separate them for recycling, do so. But a growing number of communities make it much easier, accepting all paper, mixed.

CHILDREN'S CAR SEATS

The time to think about passing a kid's car seat to another user is when you buy it, probably the last thing you have in mind at time of purchase. But if, unlike the offspring, you are anal retentive, make sure to save the original carton and complete instructions for securing the seat. Assuming the seat has not been involved in a wreck and all the original attachments and straps are in place, and assuming it's not an old model declared unsafe, the seat is okay for reuse.

Green way to reuse a child's car seat: Pass it along to family or friends.

Getting rid of an open bottle of this familiar laundry liquid should never be problem unless you're moving on short notice. Above all, don't toss a bottle of bleach in the garbage can.

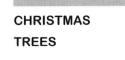

CHLORINE BLEACH

Green way to get rid of laundry bleach: Plan ahead. Use it up. If that doesn't work, give the surplus to a neighbor. If that doesn't work, flush it down the toilet. Flush again to further dilute. However, if you're on a septic system, don't use this method: Big shots of antiseptics like chlorine bleach will temporarily wipe out the bacteria that power a septic system. The only remaining alternative is to deliver the bleach to the household hazardous waste collection program in your community.

The final "Ho! Ho!" of the holidays used to be the garbage crew's heave-ho of the Christmas tree into the collection truck. But the popularity of artificial trees has stretched the average life cycle of the Christmas tree years beyond a few weeks in December and early January. Today, with millions of plastic trees stored in the at-

CHRISTMAS TREES

tic for reuse, and millions more natural trees ground into landscaping mulch after the holidays, we're doing pretty well at keeping Christmas trees of both kinds out of the landfill.

That leaves certain seasonal skeptics debating which tree is the better choice, environmentally speaking. You could say the public has spoken at the marketplace. According to the National Christmas Tree Association, a trade group representing tree growers, about 9.3 million American households purchased an artificial tree in 2006 versus 28.6 million that bought a natural tree. Real trees have held this 3-to-1 lead since 2004.

Deciding between a real Christmas tree and plastic so depends on household circumstances and tradition that third-party opinion is almost pointless. But I'll fire a shot across the balsam bough: Environmental experts say that real trees are more earth-friendly. They point out that Christmas trees are grown like crops; they're renewable. While growing, they generate oxygen and absorb carbon dioxide. They smell good in your house (that's not a scientific finding) and can be converted to good use when the season's over. Artificial trees, on the other hand, are made with petroleum—a nonrenewable resource—and are virtually unrecyclable. I rest my case.

Green way to get rid of a Christmas tree: If it's plastic and has worn out its welcome, take it completely apart and dump the remains into the garbage can. Plastic is forever and mostly nontoxic in a landfill—those fake pine branches will remain intact for a thousand years. If it's a real tree and your community offers a tree-mulching program, put it out for collection or drop it off at the mulching site.

CLOTHING

Everybody knows what you do with old clothes—you do anything to avoid throwing them away. Little kids outgrow clothes so quickly their togs are first-class hand-me-downs to friends and relatives. Teens becoming adult size are pretty good providers to their parents. But the clothing exchange begins to slow as you grow older. Shirts, sweaters, suits, and slacks start to pack closets and garment bags. What to do?

Maybe you keep a Goodwill bag in the closet, or a Salvation Army or Amvets bag. Maybe your charitable instincts begin closer to home—I've raided my son's bag of clothing castoffs many times.

Green way to get rid of clothing: Give away for reuse locally. Winter coat collections in the fall are a great example. Periodically, probe the inner reaches of closets and drawers. "If you haven't worn it in two years, you never will." I heard that somewhere and it's true. Donate unnecessary clothing to local charities for free distribution or low-cost sale in local thrift shops. In other words, take care of your brothers and sisters at home first.

**COFFEE
GROUNDS**

Coffee grounds are "the cleanest garbage around," says The Master Composter. "Spent coffee grounds are a fruit nut that has been ground and had boiling water poured through it. It isn't medical waste, or something that has been in someone's mouth." So it's okay to do something *good* with your coffee grounds—suggestions follow. If your household doesn't produce enough grounds for a reuse plan, ask the Starbucks manager for a bucketful. As part of its social responsibility, Starbucks prefers to give its grounds to local gardeners rather than dump them in the trash.

Green way to get rid of coffee grounds: As every gardener knows, coffee grounds are good for plants and soil. Grounds are rich in nitrogen. Like sand, they help break up and aerate soil. Got a compost pile or worm bin? Be their barista and give 'em a latte. But if your only choice is to dispose of coffee grounds, opt for washing them down the kitchen sink through a disposer so that the grounds get into the sewage treatment system—the reason is explained at the entry "Food Waste." But don't wash coffee grounds down a sink without a disposer—you may clog the drain pipe.

For more detail about good uses for coffee grounds, see these websites:

- www.mastercomposter.com/survey/coffee/ html
- www.sustainableenterprises.com/Business/ coffeefert.htm
- www.starbucks.com/aboutus/compost.asp

CONFIDENTIAL PAPERS

These include bank statements, tax returns, credit card bills, hospital bills, love letters, college transcripts—things you want to keep absolutely private. With identity theft a national pastime, many people routinely shred all confidential papers. That could be overkill. If you have complete control of your garbage, meaning the can remains in sight until it's dumped into the collection truck, there's hardly any risk that prying eyes will steal your Social Security and checking account numbers, according to people familiar with trash collection. Garbage truck workers are too busy dumping cans and staying safe to pay attention to the trash stream—about all that gets plucked out is an occasional Teddy Bear to decorate the truck. Your secrets are safe with the Sanitation Department.

Snooping by third parties is something else: Your trash may put you at a disadvantage in the hands of someone with malice in mind. And you can't cry foul—when you place your trash at the curb, you abandon property rights, courts generally have ruled (that's why, when you throw incriminating papers into the trash bin, it's so important to watch the receptacle until it's tipped into the collection truck).

Green way to get rid of confidential papers: Okay, shred them at home. Use the shreds to pack fragile gifts. At the same time, start reducing the volume of confidential paper you must deal with by converting bills and statements to online delivery. Otherwise, take your pick of these disposal options:

1. **The Papal Procedure.** When cardinals gather to elect a pope, they burn the ballots. This may not work if you don't have a fireplace.
2. **The Flush.** Paper torn into small pieces will flush down the toilet. You've seen this in movies. Could be tedious if you're ditching many papers. Could jam the john.
3. **Self-Destruction.** Eat your sensitive papers. Spies do it all the time.
4. **Chicken Confidential.** In a plastic bag, combine confidential papers with leftover chicken. Fish also works. Seal bag and set out to ripen. Discard with trash. The aroma will attract wildlife but repel snoops.

See the section "Bird-Cage Liner."

**CONSTRUCTION
DEBRIS**

If you've built a house or remodeled, you know that building sites are messy. The process produces left-overs—stubs of studs, odd pieces of drywall, hunks of metal, and stacks of cardboard delivery boxes. A new 2,300-square-foot house produces about 8 tons of debris, and 80% of it is reusable or recyclable.

Green way to dispose of construction debris: Get a commitment from the builder to reduce disposal to absolute minimum. Flatten corrugated boxes and deliver to the community recycling station. Bundle usable wood scraps and place them at the curb with a "FREE" sign atop, or get them to a school wood-working shop that can use the cutoffs in class projects. Take all the odd pieces of metal to a scrap yard. In a remodeling job, donate the intact, reusable fixtures such as toilets, sinks, and cabinets to a reuse center. Call Habitat for Humanity for guidance.

Finally, you can reduce the amount of drywall you send to the dump by fitting the cutoffs into wall cavities—obviously, before the finished wall is nailed to studs. If there's nothing else in the wall cavity such as wiring, plumbing, or heating, filling the empty space with drywall both reduces your disposal bill and may reduce sound transmission through the wall because the drywall is dense. And it's fire resistant.

Don't flush it down the drain—cooking oil clogs sewers. Don't pour it into the garbage can—cooking oil can seep into groundwater around a landfill.

COOKING OIL

Green way to get rid of cooking oil: Check to see if your city or town has a collection program. Many municipalities do. Those several gallons of oil remaining after you've deep-fat-fried a turkey will be recycled as biodiesel fuel for motor vehicles. You can even buy a kit for converting cooking oil into motor fuel at home. But you'll have to eat a lot of turkey to keep the $5,000 kit perking.

If no other disposal option is available, pouring liquid cooking oil into a highly absorbent medium like cat litter will help to keep the oil from migrating when it's dumped in a landfill.

CORRUGATED CARDBOARD BOXES

If you want to know how the national economy is doing, keep track of the number of corrugated cardboard boxes that pass through your household. You'll be in good company—even Federal Reserve Chairman Ben Bernanke counts boxes (okay, his staff do the counting and slip him notes while he's testifying on Capitol Hill). The volume of boxes used to ship products is a barometer of manufacturing activity. More boxes means more factory output to satisfy stronger consumer demand (picture the UPS guy ringing your doorbell).

Recovery and reuse of corrugated cardboard boxes is standard practice in business and industry. More than 70% of used cardboard boxes get into the recycling loop, including bales of old boxes shipped to China for remanufacturing into new containers for packing consumer goods shipped back to the United States.

Green way to get rid of corrugated cardboard boxes: Recycle. Most towns that offer curbside collection of recyclables also collect clean, flattened boxes. If that's not an option where you live, perhaps you can tote your boxes to the supermarket and drop them at the back room for recycling with the hundreds of cartons that pass through stores every week.

Worst way to get rid of old cardboard boxes: Bury them in a landfill, where they occupy a lot of valuable space for a very long time.

DIAPERS

Diapers were the battle zone of the 1990s that plastic water bottles are today. Back then, in the Golden Years of recycling, many new parents felt they had to apologize for using disposable diapers, which the critics held up (so to speak) as arch examples of a throw-away society. Lawmakers introduced bills banning disposables, but no laws were ever adopted. The campaign for washable, reusable diapers never got close to turning very strong consumer preference for disposables. Procter & Gamble, Kimberly-Clark, and smaller producers already had 80% market share. Today, well more than 90% of all little darlings are wrapped in disposables rather than cloth.

Manufacturers deserve credit, however, for improvements in design that both keep baby bottoms drier and reduce the bulk of diapers in landfills. This is high-tech stuff involving fancy polymers and molecules in thinner diapers that "hold the load" (a term of art) as baby perambulates.

Green way to dispose of a diaper: Honestly, there's no green way. Your only option is the garbage bin, and from there to the landfill. If you can, flush solids down the toilet. As explained at "Food Waste," it's better to run organic waste through the sewage treatment system than bury it in a landfill. If you still want to use cloth diapers and believe there's scientific proof for doing so, type this route into your browser: www.ilea.org/lcas/franklin1992.html.

DOG POOP

Of course dog poop goes in the trash, right next to Junior's deposits. The question about fecal matter in the waste stream is how much methane gas it releases to the atmosphere—methane is a serious global warmer. To get really fancy you might run a side-by-side comparison of fecal methane produced in a landfill, an incinerator, and a wastewater treatment plant. At the entry "Food Waste" in this book, you can see that sewage treatment plants are pretty good at capturing methane. If only you could train your dog to use the toilet.

Green way to get rid of dog poop: Carry a post-hole digger when you walk the dog. As necessary, dig a foot-deep hole, deposit poop, refill hole, replace divot. More likely alternative: Pick up poop using the hand-in-plastic-bag procedure. Drop into trash can.

DRAIN CLEANERS

Drain cleaning products contain chemicals that dissolve grease and break through clogged pipes—strong chemicals like sodium hydroxide or potassium hydroxide, sodium hypochlorite, and hydrochloric acid. If you would rather not keep these assertive substances in the house, try opening clogged drains with a plunger. Then flush with boiling water. Follow up with a mixture of one-quarter cup baking soda and two ounces of vinegar. Repeat as necessary.

Green way to get rid of drain cleaners: Use them up—clean those drains again! Double-check to make sure the container is empty, and replace the lid or cap before discarding in the trash. The residue of corrosive chemicals in these containers makes them unwelcome in recycling programs.

DRUGS

(Pharmaceuticals)

Green way to get rid of prescription drugs: If your community has a take-back program, use it. Otherwise, dump the pills loose—out of the bottle—into the trash, and dispose of the bottle separately so nobody pawing through your discards can associate odd pills with a label. The Office of National Drug Control Policy is even more cautious, suggesting that you mix loose pills with some undesirable substance like used kitty litter and bag this smelly mess in a sealable bag. Ugh. In general, the best place for discarded prescription drugs is a landfill, where they are some distance removed from groundwater. That's not the case when drugs are flushed down the toilet, and the drug control office warns against flushing unless the label or patient information specifically says it's an okay disposal method. But be-

cause there are so few such cases, assume that flushing isn't an option.

The egg carton in our refrigerator is one of those light gray, coarsely molded containers that you instantly know is made of recycled paper fiber, probably old newspapers. "100% recyclable carton made from 100% reclaimed paper," says a line on the label. If all egg cartons were made that way, disposal would be easy.

EGG CARTONS

Green way to get rid of an egg carton: If it's made of paper, and if your recycling collection program permits you to mix all paper, toss it in with the newspapers, magazines, and junk mail. If it's made of plastic, recycling options are very limited. You'll probably have to trash it.

"E-waste" is the broad term describing those growing heaps of electronic items that no longer keep pace with our lifestyles—cell phones that can't surf the Web, TVs

E-WASTE

that don't receive high-def signals, desktop and laptop computers too slow for new software, VCRs gathering dust on the bottom shelf, things like that. Life cycles move fast in electronics. Cell phones are cute and cuddly until they reach the terrible twos. Computers age with each new and improved operating system. Even your faithful family TV in the two-ton oak veneer cabinet now stands in the way of progress. ("Sorry, old pal"—grunt, groan—"you're outta here.") Welcome to the stunning new HDTV flat-screen!

People who study household trash say that e-waste is the fastest growing segment—and one of the most dangerous to inflict on Mother Earth. When the cathode ray tube of an old TV or computer monitor is crushed into a landfill, several pounds of lead are sprung from the glass tube. When the rechargeable batteries in laptops and cell phones are cracked open during disposal, nickel-cadmium and lithium are set free to roam. Still other nasties lurk inside electronics, and none of them should get into the air or water. Yet they can via landfill disposal or reckless recycling.

But you say, "I haven't discarded a piece of electronic gear in ages!" Just wait, you will soon. The U.S.

Environmental Protection Administration says that 460 million electronic products were put into storage (garage, attic, basement) or reuse during 2005. Sooner or later, most will be disposed of. The Consumer Electronics Association says U.S. households discard 300-million-plus pieces of electronic equipment every year, about one per person—and two-thirds of discards are still in working order.

The purpose of this section of *Green House* is to be your guide to responsible, triple-green disposal of household electronics. "Responsible" almost always means reuse, or recovery of recyclable materials using environmentally sound methods. Disposal of electronics never, ever means throwing them in the trash.

E-WASTE

Cell Phones

You have good, easy options for getting your old cell phone into a new user's hands. If you live in California or New York state you probably know what those options are—your state requires phone companies to provide a cell phone collection service.

But wherever you live, you will probably decide on a reuse or buy-back option soon. According to The Wireless Association, 80% of the U.S. population has a cell phone and the proportion is steadily increasing. In 2007, new subscribers were enrolling at the rate of 1.2 million per month. Combine this near-saturation level with the average two-year life cycle of a cell phone and you have lots of cell phones passing from original user to new user—or the garbage can, or the dresser drawer—every day.

Green way to get rid of a cell phone: First, remove all personal info from memory. Your cell phone manual should tell how. Then, contribute the cell phone for reuse or recycling. Your first stop for ideas and an action plan can be this web page maintained by the U.S. EPA: www.epa.gov/epaoswer/ hazwaste/ recycle/ecycling/donate.htm. The EPA site provides current lists and links for donating and recycling computers and cell phones, as well as links to manufacturers' asset recovery, trade-in, and leasing programs.

If you'd like to get a little cash for your old cell phone, type "cash for cell phone" into your Web browser and you'll find some contacts. To make a

*charitable contribution of your old cell phone,
type—you guessed it—"charitable donation of cell
phone." One such site is www.charitablerecycling
.com/CR/home2.asp.*

As you read this, tens of thousands of old TV sets are
being hauled out of living rooms and family rooms and
placed in temporary storage (garage, basement, out-
house) as new HDTVs (high-definition TVs) move in. The
reason for the massive retirement of old Sonys, Pana-
sonics, and the rest is more than sales promotions at
Best Buy and Wal-Mart. Federal law requires TV broad-
casters beginning in February 2009 to stop transmitting
an analog signal and broadcast only a digital signal, the
one that powers an HDTV set. Half of U.S. households
will have an HDTV by 2009, says the Consumer Electronics Association. This is a huge change and it's expected to produce mountains of trashed old TVs unless
we all get smart about better disposal options.

It's possible to keep the old TV humming if you
hook it up to cable or a satellite dish and fit it with a
special signal converter. Still, you'll know you're behind

E-WASTE
TV Sets

the times, and you'll be strongly tempted to buy a big HDTV to brag about. Millions of American consumers are expected to evict the old TV—the forecast numbers of discards is staggering. The U.S. Census says that in 2004 the average household had 2.5 TV sets in use; nationwide, about 268 million. And that was before the big shift to HDTV began. Even if only 20% of old TVs are trashed, the number is 54 million. The potential for lead and other hazards leaching out of crushed TVs into groundwater is sobering.

Green way to deal with an old TV: Don't dump it, put it to good reuse within your household. For example, the big console TV can be combined with the VCR and DVD players in a new mini-theater used exclusively for watching movies or playing video games.

Smaller TVs can be used as monitors in a home security system—you can keep an eye on the front door, back door, backyard, and garage with the addition of wireless cameras and a few auxiliary gizmos.

If reuse of the old TV at home simply won't

work, your strategy is to buy time. Store the old TV in some out-of-the-way place until your community sponsors a collection program for old electronics. And when it does, ask the organizers where the TVs and desktops will be shipped. The best destination is a de-manufacturing plant somewhere stateside for recovery of reusable components and disposal of the remainder in an environmentally friendly manner. (Reality check: Such plants are few. Most TV sets that are not landfilled will probably board a slow boat to China, Africa, or India, where poor people hack out re-sellable metals and circuit boards and dump what's left in the river. The Chinese government it-self says that 70% of the world's e-waste lands in China.)

Sony, in cooperation with Waste Management, offers a free take-back program for Sony TVs as well as other Sony electronics. Other makes will be ac-cepted for a small fee—inquire. By phone: 877-439-2795. Or try this website: www.wm.com/sony. Also, you may be able to find a TV drop-off point nearby using this link: www.Mygreenelectronics.org. Or take a look at the Best Buy site: http://communications

.bestbuy.com/communityrelations/recyclingevents
.asp.

E-WASTE

Computers and
Hard Drives

It used to be a real challenge to get rid of an old laptop or desktop without bruising the environment or hanging your hard-drive out for all the world to see. If you were worried that some of those dirty deals still lurked in long-term memory, personally tossing the PC into the landfill or incinerator probably was a good idea, if not environmentally correct. But it's getting easier to be both "clean" and green with computers. All the big brand-name producers now offer take-back programs they claim are totally secure or, as one enthusiastic Best Buy staffer told me, "We'll shred the hard drive before your very eyes!"—wearing goggles, of course.

Following are addresses for the take-back programs of major manufacturers and retailers, listed in this order: Apple, Dell, Gateway, Hewlett-Packard, IBM, Toshiba, Best Buy, and Circuit City.

- www.apple.com/environment/recycling/
- www.dell.com/content/topics/segtopic.aspx/
  dell_recycling?c=us&cs=19&l=en&s=dhs

- http://gateway.eztradein.com/gateway/
- www.hp.com/hpinfo/globalcitizenship/
  environment/return/index.html
- www-03.ibm.com/financing/us/recovery/
  index.html
- www.toshibadirect.com/td/b2c/ebtext.to?
  page=reuse&seg=HHO
- http://communications.bestbuy.com/
  communityrelations/recycling.asp
- http://cc.eztradein.com/cc/

If you'd rather not type in those long addresses, go to the one listed below. It's maintained by the City of Fort Collins, Colorado. For the convenience of residents, Fort Collins has gathered all the URLs listed above as quick links, all in one place.

- http://fcgov.com/recycling/computers-
  recycle.php

What about donating your old computer for charitable use? I don't recommend doing that, for two reasons: first, to avoid the risk of passing along personal information in computer memory, even if you're absolutely certain nothing remains there; and second, to acknowledge that computer hand-me-downs don't do any favors for anyone. A person who needs a computer but can't afford one should get a state-of-the-art system. Rather than pass along old gear, make a cash contribution to the charity for purchase of new computer equipment.

Green way to get rid of your old laptop, desktop, and monitor: Deliver to a take-back program like one of those listed above, or to another reputable recycling program. If you work in a large office, it may be possible for you to add your home system to the inventory of desktops periodically shipped to a commercial recycler when new office desktops and monitors arrive. For security, companies want a paper trail on their discarded gear, from the moment it's loaded on the truck to final disassembly of circuit boards and the rest of the parts. (A typical desktop contains almost an ounce of gold in various circuit boards plus bits of platinum and silver.)

To learn more about commercial recycling pro-

grams, take a look at the website of one company in the business, Intercon Solutions, based in Chicago Heights, Illinois: www.interconsolutions.com.

E-WASTE

Keyboards, Printers, Scanners, and Fax Machines

It seems a shame to trash these things. That's why so many pile up in closets and back rooms. Even if they're in working condition, old computer keyboards, printers, scanners, and fax machines have very little prospect of reuse. There's a reason that businesses write off this stuff in a couple of years. Intercon Solutions, the company listed at "Computers and Hard Drives" in this section, observes candidly at its website that "most types of consumer electronics actually have a negative value, meaning that the costs involved with processing are not offset by the value of the raw material." Or as one observer puts it, printers, keyboards, and such are "pure crap."

Green way to get rid of keyboards, printers, scanners, and fax machines: Store them until your community has a collection program.

My black inkjet cartridge sent me a remarkable message one morning. Instead of the usual "YOU *!!X%#@ DUMMY, I'M DRY!" it was a gentle prompt including useful advice. "Black ink is low," it purred. "You can print black by combining the other colors." I was speechless. What had happened to my blinking old inkjet tyrant?

Maybe, finally, my printer was having mercy on a poor, humble user who often must choose between eating and replacing printer cartridges. Why do computer *printers* cost so little? Because printer *inkjets* run dry so often and cost so much.

Green way to get rid of an inkjet cartridge: Don't get rid of it; refill it. You can do it at home with a re-filling kit, but that's a messy routine. Better, I think, is to patronize a local specialist in this business. There's one in my town and she does a great job. Refills are cheap compared to buying brand-name or third-party replacements. In general, refills and third-party replacement inkjets have almost the same capacity as brand-names but do less well on permanence (see the PC World article reference below).

If you're squeamish about replacing brand-name original equipment with anything else and must dispose of an old cartridge, try to get it into a household hazardous waste collection program. To find a nearby program, go to www.earth911.org. But don't worry if you do have to trash the old cartridge. A study reported in the Commonwealth of Australia Gazette *says that printer ink "is not considered to pose a risk to the environment."*

Still looking for a refiller? Type "inkjet refill service" into your Web browser.

And to learn more about third-party ink cartridges for brand-name printers, take a look at this article online from PC World: http://pcworld.about .com/magazine/2109p022id111767.htm.

Green way to dispose of an old VCR or DVD player: Marry them to the old TV in a mini–home theater, as suggested at "TV Sets," above.

E-WASTE

VCRs and DVDs

E-WASTE

iPhones, iPods, MP3 Players, and PDAs

Original owners keep these items only a short time before replacing with new ones, according to industry analysts. This may not be your experience but, for example, an iPod is replaced after about a year and a half. What then? Friends and family often inherit; some units are just thrown away.

Green way to get rid of an iPhone, iPod, MP3 player, or PDA: Pass it along to another user. Or list it on eBay or Craigslist. Take the usual precautions about cleaning out all personal info stored in memory. If the unit is truly kaput, see that the battery is removed for proper handling (see "Batteries"), and toss.

EYEGLASSES

Lions Clubs International is the world leader in eyeglass recycling. To donate old specs, contact your local club. Principal recycling centers are listed at www.lionsclubs .org/EN/content/vision_eyeglass_centers.shtml#.

The issue is litter—clam shells, paper bags, ketchup pouches, napkins, sandwich wraps, drink cups, all simply pitched out the car window. That's what makes people mad about fast-food trash. This is a twist on the proverb "Out of sight, out of mind." If we never observed fast-food wrappings along the highway, we'd just praise the lord and pass the french fries.

FAST-FOOD CONTAINERS AND DELI BOXES

Green way to get rid of fast-food containers: Toss them in the trash and quit worrying. They're a very small proportion of consumer waste—"less than one-third of one percent of dump deposits," says William L. Rathje, the University of Arizona anthropologist known for his excavations of garbage dumps.

Polishing is such a virtuous activity, it's hard to believe that polish contains hazardous ingredients like diethylene glycol, petroleum distillates, and nitrobenzene. I've read about a nonhazardous, homemade polish: one part lemon juice to two parts olive oil. Leftovers can be poured on the salad.

FLOOR AND FURNITURE POLISH

Green way to get rid of floor and furniture polish containers: Because of the hazardous residues, don't toss them into the trash. Some communities—not many—will collect these containers along with recyclable bottles and cans. Otherwise, you may have to set them aside for delivery to the household hazardous waste drop-off station nearest to you. Find the nearest station at www.earth911.org.

FOOD WASTE

Next time conversation drags, pop this question to your group: Is it better for the environment if you flush food waste down the kitchen sink through a disposer-grinder; or is it better if you toss those pizza crusts, coffee grounds, apple cores, lettuce leaves, and other food scraps into the garbage can? Even if you don't have the kitchen-sink option at your place, just suppose that you do—this is leading to a point about global warming.

Garbage can. Most food scraps get tossed into the garbage can. In fact, that's the only place for bones, shells, fruit pits, corn husks, and fibrous materials that can jam food grinders. In the U.S., food scraps represent about 12% of the weight of a typical household garbage bag (paper is the largest proportion at 34%). Some garbage bags are burned in an incinerator, producing carbon dioxide, the big daddy of global warming gases. However, most household garbage bags are buried in a landfill, where the food scraps and other organic wastes like diapers and pet poop slowly decompose, producing methane gas, another important cause of global warming. Some landfills capture the methane and use it to power turbines producing electricity, but much methane escapes into the atmosphere, adding to that warming effect.

Kitchen drain. Food waste that runs through the grinder in your kitchen sink enters the sewer pipe, mixes with bathroom and laundry waste from your dwelling, and begins a long underground journey to the community sewage treatment plant. Getting there is easy—the stuff is 98% water and only 2% solids, including all those kitchen scraps. At the treatment plant, if it's a modern one like the Hyperion plant in Los Angeles, the solids are placed in "digesters" where bacteria convert much of the solid material into methane gas, the same global warming gas produced in a landfill. But the big difference in a state-of-the-art sewage treatment plant is that the methane is captured and used to power the plant or run an electric generator. Comparatively little methane escapes to do environmental damage.

But wait, there's still another advantage to the kitchen-drain route. When the sewage treatment process ends, what's left is a large volume of water, called effluent, and a large volume of solids, called sludge. The effluent should be clean enough after treatment to use for irrigation or to discharge into a river or lake without threatening public health. Sometimes it's further purified into perfectly drinkable water, though people don't line up for samples. Sewage sludge is a totally different story. Sludge is packed with nutrients. It makes things grow and is good for the soil. Properly treated sludge is a manufactured product of enormous value. Probably the best known sludge product is Milwaukee's Milorganite brand, which generations of gardeners have used to nurture flowers and veggies.

Green way to get rid of food waste: Environmentally speaking, the best way to dispose of food waste is to send it into the sewer system via your food waste disposer in the kitchen sink.

Finally, applause for folks who dispose of old veggies (but no meats or oils) in their home compost pile or community yard-waste collection program, and to those who feed family pets with leftovers. A dog I know slightly has a great fondness for yellow and red peppers—oddly, not for green.

FURNITURE

Imagine the sagging, soiled, sorry remains of a humongous sofa sitting at the curb, absorbing rainwater and insult. Furniture like this often gets tossed in a two-step—first to the covered porch for final rites, which can last more than a year; then to the street, waiting for decent burial. And it's okay to inter old couches and upholstered chairs in a landfill. The cloth, wire, wood, metal, and stuffing aren't hazardous and don't occupy much space after they're crushed and compacted by bulldozers.

But as for all other furniture—tables, wooden and metal chairs, bookcases, bed frames, dressers, desks, etc.—there's never good reason to trash them, so long as they're in one piece and even if you do have access to someone else's dumpster.

Green way to get rid of surplus furniture: Family members have first claim, of course. Organizations like the Salvation Army and Goodwill Industries will accept your delivery of furniture in good condition. To contribute your reusable furniture to a needy household, try contacting a community church or social service agency. Or just put it at the curb with a "FREE" sign on. If you do use the street as your agency, be thoughtful and cover furniture with a clear plastic sheet to protect against weather.

GLASS BOTTLES

Those were the days . . .

Until the 1960s, most beverages were delivered in refillable glass bottles. The milkman left a quart at your doorstep and collected the empty on his next stop. The beer and soft drink route drivers unloaded cases of product at the supermarket and you paid a 2-cent deposit on each bottle, enough incentive those days to get almost all the empties back to the store so that a high-school kid could earn a little money sorting them in the back room. It was a simple system—and long ago. Today, hardly any glass beverage bottles are refilled in the

United States (although they still are abroad—in France, according to industry sources, the average wine bottle gets refilled up to eight times before saying adieu).

Glass bottles of all kinds have steadily lost U.S. market share to aluminum, plastic, and waxed paper containers. Convenience and cost are the big factors. People just don't want to haul empty bottles back to the store, bottlers don't want to haul heavy glass containers (and lose some to breakage), and retailers don't want to devote space and time to sorting and returning bottles.

Okay, if refilling glass bottles is history, how about recycling, turning old glass into new glass? Nine or 10 states use deposit systems to encourage recycling, and the results are impressive. Iowa and Vermont report redemption rates of 93%! But nationally, glass container recycling in the United States scores the lowest on the planet—about 25%, says the Glass Packaging Institute. While we hang our heads in shame, let us reflect on the environmental goodness of recycled glass. It saves natural resources, uses only a fraction of the energy of bottle-making from silica sand, reduces carbon dioxide emissions, and has an unlimited life—glass can be recycled over and over and over again.

Green way to get rid of a glass bottle: The choice is to recycle it or trash it. Ironically, in many parts of the United States today, there's little difference. Because market rates for recovered glass are so low (as low as $10 a ton), it often costs the recycling program more to haul glass to a bottle plant than to bury it in a landfill. Some curbside recycling service managers privately wish they could keep glass out of the recycling bin altogether, but glass recycling is too deeply embedded for that. At least the environmental risk of landfilling is low. Glass is inert, no threat to groundwater. Buried in a landfill it just sits there, forever, waiting for an archeologist several thousand years hence to dig it up and exclaim, "It's Miller time!"

GLUE

Bottle-bottom remnants of water-soluble glue, such as Elmer's Glue-All, can be thrown in the trash without concern. But glue containing petroleum-based solvents like trichloroethane and toluene—rubber cement, for example—requires special handling.

Green way to get rid of non-water-soluble glue: Assuming what you have is beyond use by anyone else, do your part for the ozone layer: Save the glue for collection by a household hazardous waste disposal program.

Garage and machine-shop grease is disposed of like motor oil—see page 78. Used vegetable oil, the stuff you deep-fat-fried the turkey in, needs other procedures, described at page 37. This entry concerns animal fat—goose grease, bacon grease, chicken fat, all those greases that turn solid at room temperature. Animal fat may clog kitchen pipes but presents no other special disposal problem, either in a sewage treatment plant or a landfill. The main idea is to prevent leftover cooking grease from soaking into other household disposables that can be recycled, like paper and cardboard.

GREASE

Green way to get rid of grease: Collect it in a can that you keep in the refrigerator, use it in cooking when possible, and toss the congealed surplus in the trash.

**HOME-OFFICE
PAPER**

Almost everyone now accepts the principle that computer technology doesn't replace paper, it multiplies paper. Those stacks of printouts around your 18 by 18 inch work surface in front of the computer screen represent exciting new ideas and adventures. You never imagined that one day you'd need to buy home-office copy paper by the case.

But sooner or later, the ideas, agreements, and contracts are fully mature and stored neatly on the hard drive, easy to recall when necessary. The paper is surplus.

Green way to get rid of home-office paper: Curbside collection programs are beginning to combine all paper. If you're accustomed to separating home-office paper and would rather not expose it to inferior grades like newspaper and cereal boxes, consider whether you can merge your office-grade paper with the recycling program at work (taking care to exclude confidential papers).

This little sermon applies to fungicides, pesticides, and insecticides. Among all the chemicals used around the house, this threesome is the most treacherous. One big problem, say people who worry about it professionally, is the lack of warning in large type concerning the possible health risks from coming in contact with the "-cides." The warning on a pack of cigarettes is much easier to read and understand.

Here are two simple rules: First, use these products as if they cause cancer. Second, never throw an "empty" container in the trash; you can't tell conclusively that it's empty, and the risk of residues getting into underground water via the landfill is simply too great.

INSECTICIDES

Green way to dispose of the "–cides": With products like these, the green approach begins at point of purchase. Calculate your needs very carefully and then ratchet down a notch or two. If there's a small size, buy it. It's better to run out than run over. If you're stuck with leftovers, try giving them to another user. Your fallback option is to set the product aside for delivery to the community hazardous waste collection site. Local government officials will know where and when. In rural areas, the county agricultural office should have information. End of sermon.

INSULATION

You know insulation as the fiberglass fluff placed inside walls and between floors, and wrapped around pipes. If you have insulation on your hands it must be left over from a construction project.

Green way to get rid of insulation: Don't get rid of it—stuff it. If you have access to wall and floor cavities in your basement, or attic, or a crawlspace, you'll probably see opportunities to use leftovers. Remember that insulation can reduce transmission of sound as well as heat. But for heaven's sake, don't discard insulation. Give it away to another builder. Insulation is long-lasting, nonpolluting, and beneficial—a rare combination.

Junk is in the eye of the beholder. You see unsolicited mail as a plague. I see those catalogs, credit card offers, and travel brochures as interesting reflections of the marketplace. I at least scan every piece of advertising mail delivered to my place. It confirms my position as a gold-plated member of the Greatest Consumer Society on Earth. When I complain about getting catalogs from Nordstrom, Saks, and L.L. Bean, I'm actually making a statement about lifestyle.

JUNK MAIL

I like my cousin Steve's approach. His route back from the mailbox goes past the paper recycling bin, where he quickly sorts the delivery into winners (those pieces go into the house) and losers (straight into the bin). It takes only a few seconds.

Some days, I admit, there's an awful lot of non-personal mail in the box. On a late October day, at the peak of the pre-Christmas catalog mailing season, there were 33 pieces in the box: one party invitation; two bills; one piece of personal correspondence containing a newspaper clipping inscribed "Thought you'd like to see"; three each of newsletters and magazines; and 23 catalogs. That was a record at our place—and a direct result of our shopping habits: To save time and travel expense (car, gasoline, traffic jams, parking), we buy lots of stuff by mail. Our name gets on mailing lists. But back on topic—how to get your name off mailing lists and reduce the volume of unwanted mail . . .

Green way to get rid of (much) junk mail: This is not a 100% certain solution. Putting your name and address on a mailing list is a big industry that never sleeps. But you can take some steps to cut the volume. Step 1 is to go to the website of Privacy Rights Clearinghouse, a San Diego nonprofit organization: www.privacyrights.org/fs/fs4-junk.htm. This will take you to "Fact Sheet 4: Reducing Junk Mail," a well-written, comprehensive, even-handed, and useful explanation of how your name gets on mailing lists and how to get it somewhat off. Among several links in the fact sheet you'll see how to register with the Mail Preference Service of the Direct Marketing Association, the trade group representing major national marketing firms. When you register, your name goes on the "Do Not Mail" file used by DMA members to police their mailing lists.

One more tactic to reduce the mailbox load: If

possible, switch your regular monthly bills to delivery online—you're probably paying the utilities online already. And sign up for electronic delivery of stock prospectuses and reports (the ones you never read anyway).

I caught a whiff of burning leaves one day last fall. And I must admit it smelled good. This was in the country, where law-abiding citizens think that some ordinances, like burn bans, are optional.

LEAVES

Landfill disposal bans are easier to enforce—about half of the states prohibit dumping of leaves and other yard wastes. The proportion of yard waste in household trash has fallen from 18% in 1990 to about 13% today, one of the more successful modifications in Americans' disposal behavior. And it makes great good sense. Why commit this stuff to a slow underground rot when you can turn it aboveground into a useful new product like mulch?

Green way to get rid of leaves: Rake them to the curb loose for vacuum collection by the municipal composting program, or bag them in paper for pickup by the composters. If your community offers neither service, request that they consider a change.

As a more radical alternative, consider composting all your yard wastes at home. This does require space and some tolerance for disorder. A compost pile can be as casual as a mound of leaves, grass, withered flowers, and vegetable tops in some obscure corner of the yard. The pile requires only air, water, occasional stirring, and time. Give it what it needs and success is virtually guaranteed. You can hasten decomposition by stirring in small amounts of dirt and leftover fertilizer. Chewing up the leaves with a lawn mower before dumping will speed things along.

See also the entry "Yard Waste."

LIGHT BULBS

You have two kinds of light bulbs to dispose of. First, the easy one, those friendly old 40-, 60-, and 100-watters—incandescent lights. They're trash when they die. Nothing hazardous resides within an incandescent light and there's no recycling market for the glass and metal.

Pretty soon, old-style bulbs will be only a memory as more and more people replace them with the far more efficient compact fluorescent lights—CFLs. Federal law is hastening the change: incandescent lights begin phasing out in 2012 and can no longer be sold in the United States after 2014.

Though it's okay to trash incandescent lights, disposing of fluorescent lights is a different matter. Is there any more delicate trash than a dead fluorescent tube? You carry it like a stick of dynamite, place it gently in the can, then stand back and throw in something heavy, hoping the light pops into harmless smithereens.

Pops, yes; harmless, no. All fluorescent lights contain mercury. When the light breaks, the mercury is released and free to wander into the air you breathe and the water you and I, and fish and dogs and cats and hippos and most critters, drink. Mercury is bad stuff for all creatures, and terribly persistent.

Yes, there are rules and regulations controlling the disposal of fluorescent lights, but they don't generally apply to households. Your castle is exempt because you are considered—nothing personal here—a "small quantity generator." You're not a Toyota factory or a Target store, with thousands of fluorescent lights burning out every year. Large quantity generators are required to ship their old fluorescent tubes to recycling plants for safe recovery of the mercury and other metals.

But wait a minute, you say. Aren't all of the millions of American households really one great big generator of burned-out fluorescent lights? That is a brilliant observation, and it will become even more brilliant as more and more households replace their old incandescent lights with those sexy little CFLs. Though they cost more than incandescents, CFLs really do save electricity, and they are alleged to last a long time.

Yet sometime soon, CFLs from households will begin multiplying in the trash—with Wal-Mart selling its own brand of CFL, that's a sure thing. And unlike those innocent old incandescent lights, growing volumes of compact fluorescent lights in household trash can pose a mercury hazard that diminishes the green gains of using less electricity.

Green way to dispose of fluorescent lights, including CFLs: Store them safely at your place until your community announces a collection program for house-

hold hazardous wastes, and then personally deliver your fluorescents into safe hands. If your community doesn't have a program, ask why.

Another option is to look for a commercial recycler of fluorescent lights. Most of the companies that handle large-quantity generators will take your old tubes and CFLs at no charge if you drop them off. Most large metro areas have at least one of these companies. Check the classified telephone directory and www.lamprecycle.org.

MAGAZINES

Magazines once were the pariah of paper collection programs because of the glue in their bindings. Now that paper is being collected mixed in many recycling programs, magazines are getting more respect. Many find their way into low-end but steady use converted into tissue paper and boxboard at paper mills in the Far East.

Green way to get rid of magazines—even National Geographic: *Leave them in your doctor's waiting room, where old magazines never die.*

MATTRESSES

Green way to get rid of a mattress: Assuming it's clean and intact, try to pass it along to another user. Post free on Craigslist, for example, or contact freecycle.org, or call the Salvation Army. Exhaust all reuse alternatives before you place it out for collection with the trash.

METAL (ODD BITS)

"A piece of old Yankee advice," an old Yankee said on apt occasions. "Never throw away a piece of metal." We've kept the faith, moving a collection of metal from place to place, and we've never lacked the odd screw, bolt, nail, spring, angle iron, flat plate, or hunk of pipe. Save it all—you never know when you'll need it. Just a piece of old Yankee advice.

MILK AND JUICE CARTONS

Milk and juice cartons are tough to recycle and not acceptable in most collection programs. The problem is the way they're made—an inside wall of paper covered by plastic film on both sides. Separating the layers costs too much to make recovery of the paper fiber feasible.

(The same goes for aseptic cartons.) But you may be fortunate to live in one of the places where so-called gable-top cartons are collected and sent to market. Check with your municipal services office. People with strong artsy-craftsy genes can think of all sorts of secondary uses for milk and juice cartons, like making containers for growing herbs. But you can also just flatten empty cartons and toss them in the trash.

Glass bottles and food jars are recyclable. But mirrors, glass cookware, glass goblets, window panes, and most other non-container glass are not the same kind of glass—they don't fall neatly into glass recyclers' melting pots.

MIRRORS AND MISCELLANEOUS GLASS

Green way to get rid of non-container glass: If the glass items are usable, include them in your next trek to the local reuse store. If not, throw them in the trash. They don't occupy much space in a landfill, and there's no environmental hazard.

MOTOR OIL

If you are a DIY guy or gal—a do-it-yourself motor oil changer—you enjoy sliding under the engine, wrenching off the plug, and feeling the lubricant run around your fingers into the catching pan. Changing the oil is part of a relationship; it shows you care. And you are probably young at heart. The typical DIY individual is a younger male.

After age 45, the DIY tendency drops off fast. Perhaps the romance of motor maintenance is gone; certainly the convenience of a 15-minute oil change is alluring. The proliferation of oil-change emporiums, longer-lasting motor oil, and improvements in engine efficiency all are factors. The old 3,000-mile standard for an oil change is being replaced by 5,000 miles, or more. As a result, DIY oil changing is declining fast—not a bad thing when you consider that, second to spills by the Exxon Valdez, most oil pollution of water resources can be traced back to improper disposal by a householder.

Most folks who change their own motor oil are not polluters. But the minority who are have the means to wreak havoc on nature. Some oil changers pour the old stuff on roads for "dust control." Some pour it on the ground without any reason, or down a storm sewer. Some slip it in the trash, a nice surprise for sanitation employees as jugs of oil, compressed by the garbage packer, pop open and spray the truck and the workers with hydrocarbons plus various additives, none benign and all persistent.

That's the problem with dumped motor oil: It's persistent. It finds its way back to you, usually through the water supply. (As the U.S. Environmental Protection Agency declares in a continuing campaign for proper disposal, "You dump it, you drink it.") Motor oil never wears out. It gets dirty in use, but once the dirt is removed, it can be used again with the same effectiveness as the virgin product.

Green way to get rid of motor oil: Recycle it—there's no second option. And with the price of oil running at all-time highs, recycling should be easy. Your community may have a collection program. If the Wal-Mart in your area has car-service bays, you can drop off your dirty motor oil at no charge. Ditto the oil filter. Why do most automobile service stations accept these items without dirty looks? Because dirty motor oil earns at least 25 cents a gallon these days.

If none of these suggestions works for you, follow this link to locate the nearest drop-off point: www.earth911.org.

NAIL POLISH AND POLISH REMOVER

Green way to dispose of nail polish: If the nail polish has dried solid in the bottle, toss it in the trash. But if the polish is still liquid in the bottle, set it aside for the next roundup of household hazardous waste. The same applies to nail polish remover.

NEWSPAPERS

Suppose that today is your first "green" day. Yesterday you threw all household discards into the trash can. Today you're a new you. You're revved up, ready to go—and curious. You want to know what better things you can do with your trash, better than burying in a landfill or burning in an incinerator. So, as head of the household, you assign another member to sort the trash. All plastic stuff goes in one pile, all metal in another, and so on with glass and paper of all kinds. To make this exercise truly scientific, you provide a scale so that your lab assistant can weigh each pile.

If your household is typically American, the paper pile will weigh the most. (And if yours is like most households, you are now deeply in debt to your lab assistant.) By weight, paper is the largest single category of household trash, according to the U.S. Environmental Protection Agency. And to justify this rather messy exercise, paper provides a number of elementary lessons in the economics of trash.

Consider newspaper, the most common kind of paper in household trash. Assume that the cost to dump newspaper and everything else in your trash can is $35 a ton, the national average for landfilling in 2005. Assume next that you can pull newspaper out of the trash and sell it for $70 a ton. Easy decision: You trundle that bundle of old news to the recycler, pocket $70, and save $35 in an avoided cost for a landfill burial that never happened.

But what if the recycler's warehouse is jammed? He has plenty of old newspaper and doesn't need to buy any more for a while. He'll take it off your hands but won't pay you anything. Still a better deal? Sure it is, because you're still avoiding a $35 per ton disposal fee. In fact, prices for commodities like recycled newspaper do move up and down depending on demand, including demand from faraway places like China and India. (Many boats that unload manufactured goods on the U.S. coasts are reloaded with bales of recycled paper, plastics, and metals for delivery to the Far East.)

Thirty-one percent of old newspaper is recycled as newsprint, says the paper industry. Export is the next largest category at 28%, and the remainder goes into a variety of things like cereal boxes and toilet tissue. But no matter where or how it's used, every bit of paper recovered for reuse helps to conserve forests of paperpulp trees, and despite economics that's the ultimate green objective.

Green way to get rid of newspaper: Collect it according to instructions from your community recycling program. In some places that means you keep it separate from other paper, perhaps placing newspaper in paper grocery bags. In a growing number of communities, all paper can be collected mixed, making it much easier to participate.

The active ingredient is sodium hydroxide—lye—which also is found in drain cleaners. Presumably the quantity to be disposed of is a smallish leftover not worth giving away, as a hostess gift, for example.

OVEN CLEANERS

Green way to get rid of oven cleaners: Flush down the toilet. Rinse the empty container, taking care not to splash on your hands or face. Throw the container in the trash.

You've received a very important overnight delivery. Now, what do you do with the empty container?

OVERNIGHT DELIVERY BOXES AND ENVELOPES

Green way to dispose of express delivery packaging: If it's a large box made of corrugated paper, tear off and trash whatever plastic sleeves may be stuck on the box, then merge the box in your community paper recycling program. If corrugated isn't collected by your municipality (that's hard to believe, it's so sellable), you can usually recycle it at a supermarket. Food stores routinely bundle and recycle the hundreds of food cartons they receive weekly. So do large pharmacies.

If the express package is a cardboard envelope, tear off the plastic sleeve, if any, and recycle the envelope along with empty food cartons. The express envelope and the Grape Nuts box, for example, are made of the same material.

If the express package is a flexible, lightweight envelope, it's probably made of high density polyethylene (HDPE) by DuPont under the brand name Tyvek. It's not paper but plastic, and exceedingly tough—so tough it can be used for some purpose at least one more time. At my place, HDPE envelopes are turned inside out (reach inside the envelope, grab the bottom seam, pull back to invert, smooth the wrinkles) and become mailers again. The open end can be stapled shut and is quite secure.

Incidentally, if the Tyvek brand sounds familiar, you've probably seen it wrapped around new houses under construction. The material is used to stop infiltration of wind and water.

This entry is about deliveries to your house, the packages that arrive by the U.S. Postal Service, UPS, DHL, and all the other carriers. This entry is not about bags you carry home from shopping (see "Paper and Plastic Bags," below).

You've unwrapped the delivery and retrieved whatever's inside, and you're now stuck with: the outer package, usually a corrugated cardboard box or heavy wrapping paper; the inside cushioning materials, such as crinkled newspaper, plastic peanuts, expanded polystyrene (Styrofoam) shaped like the product, plastic bags; and maybe some printed matter on office-grade paper—the instructions, warranty, etc.

Instructions concerning corrugated cardboard boxes, paper, and plastic bags appear elsewhere in this book. That leaves the packing peanuts and block forms of expanded polystyrene.

PACKAGING

Green way to dispose of packing peanuts: Bag them and deliver to either a mailing service in town or a community free-exchange site. Most UPS stores accept packing peanuts. You can also save them for your own packing/shipping needs in the future. For

*more ideas, call the Peanut Hotline at 800-828-2214
or try www.loosefillpackaging.com.*

*Now for the hard one, that big white hunk of
Styrofoam. You're grateful that the packaging has
kept the merchandise pristine in transit, but now it's
an intruder. It's made of the same material as the
packing peanuts, but the shape makes it practically
useless in any other packaging situation (except
when you repack for moving the product you just
received—consider storing it for that purpose).*

*If you live in an area where it's easy for house-
holders to recycle blocks of Styrofoam, congratula-
tions. But as the American Chemistry Council admits,
"The infrastructure needed to collect polystyrene
and sell recovered material is not sustainable in all
markets." That's putting it mildly. Hardly any municipal recycling program accepts block Styrofoam. The
problem is density—compared to newspaper, for example, or even plastic milk jugs, Styrofoam is very
light for its size. You have to collect an awful lot of
it to produce marketable quantities.*

*Advice (I won't call it green): Disposal as trash is
virtually the only option for block Styrofoam. (If you*

want to reduce the space it occupies in your trash can, place the blocks inside a big plastic bag and jump on the bag.) Landfill burial is the best resting place. EPS Recycling International, a trade group, cheerfully reports that Styrofoam "is an ideal material for landfill because it remains inert, is non-toxic, odor-free, and non-biodegradable by design." Styrofoam "provides stability within landfill sites."

PAINT

William L. Rathje, the University of Arizona anthropologist, says you can tell what kind of neighborhood you're in by looking in the garbage cans. No, he's not talking about identity theft but cultural artifacts. Rathje says that in a poor neighborhood the garbage cans contain lots of leftovers from car maintenance—empty cans of motor oil, brake fluid, and engine degunker, car-body repair kits, etc. In a wealthy neighborhood you see containers of herbicides, pesticides, and other gardening chemicals. But in a middle-class neighborhood you find every color of the American Dream—empty and near-empty cans of paint, plus gummy paint rollers and brushes stiff with rigor mortis.

Leftovers seem an inescapable part of every home painting project. Having been there myself, I think the explanation is anxiety—fear of running out of paint before you run out of wall or ceiling. The tut-tutters tell us to do a better job of estimating paint required for the job, but they've never known the terror of dashing to the paint store five minutes before closing. And we hang on to leftover paint for equally good reason, to touch up later, though that rarely happens.

Green way to get rid of paint: The best way is to avoid disposal altogether. The home strategy is to keep all partial cans of paint as a housewarming gift to the next owner of your dwelling. Pretty ribbons may add some credibility to this ruse. But the sensible strategy is to donate leftover paint while it's still usable to a free-exchange collection center in your community. If disposal is your only choice, the plan depends on whether the paint is latex (water based) or alkyd (oil based). Latex is easy: Pop open the lid and let the paint dry solid. Be patient—drying may take a while. When the paint has solidified, toss it in the trash with the lid off so that handlers can see it's

*no problem. The same approach goes for latex-cov-
ered tools like brushes and rollers—once dry they
pose no environmental hazard. But alkyd paint is a
potential hazard and must be set aside for delivery
to your community's periodic roundup of household
hazardous wastes. Fortunately, oil-based paints and
varnishes command less than 30% of the market—a
share that continues to dwindle as water-based
products become ever better.*

If you remember the time before latex paint, when
alkyd (oil based) paint was the standard, you also remember the mess and the stink of cleaning up after
painting. Getting paint off the brush and yourself
meant practically bathing in mineral spirits or turpen-
tine. If you're unlucky enough to be doing that still, remember to wear rubber gloves and take special care
with disposal.

PAINT BRUSH CLEANER AND PAINT THINNER

*Green way to deal with alkyd paint solvents: Set
them aside until the solids settle in the container,
then pour through a paper filter into a clean con-*

tainer for reuse. The accumulated sludge should be delivered to a household hazardous waste collection program.

PAINT STRIPPER

Read the label to determine whether it contains either lye or methylene chloride.

Procedure for lye: Taking care not to splash on hands or face, flush it down the drain with lots of water.

Procedure for methylene chloride: Set aside for delivery to a household hazardous waste collection program. If that's not an option in your community, think about who can use it: A house painter? A furniture refinishing shop?

PAPER AND PLASTIC BAGS

It's time for—*Jeopardy!*

The answer is "Neither."

And the question? A moment's pause before you confidently declare . . .

"Paper or plastic!"

In the best of all possible, trash-free worlds, you and I will take a reusable bag or bags on every shopping trip. The clerk's question, "Paper or plastic?" will no longer stir anxious moments in the check-out line as we mentally run a life-cycle analysis on paper versus plastic and look over our shoulder for hints of political correctness. In fact, running the numbers on paper versus plastic leads nowhere—you can make a sound argument either way. Making those arguments is beyond the scope of this book. But if you're curious, you can begin at Google with "Paper versus plastic life cycle analysis" and study everything that comes up.

In the meantime, live free: Get yourself a reusable shopping bag for every trip.

Green way to dispose of a paper or plastic bag: The green strategy is to reuse the bag at least once. Here are just a few examples: Reuse a paper grocery bag as a container for newspapers going to recycling, or as a container for other recyclables. Sturdy paper bags of all kinds also can be cut along the seams, flattened, and used as package wrappers. Plastic grocery store bags can be used again to pick up dog poop. Clean plastic bags can be used to wrap leftovers. My morning newspaper is delivered in a plastic bag bearing the printed reminder, "This bag is recyclable." We use one bag as the container and stuff it full with dozens more bags, making a plastic sausage that goes into the recycling bin every few weeks. Fortunately, our curbside collection program accepts plastic bags; otherwise, we'd take them back to the grocery store for recycling.

PETS (Deceased)

The American Veterinary Medical Association estimates that Americans own 62 million dogs, 71 million cats, 10 million birds, and 5 million horses. With other creatures added in—fish, ferrets, turtles, snakes, etc.—the total rises to about 216 million. In many households, pets enjoy parity as family members, making decisions difficult when a pet dies.

Green ways to dispose of a dead pet: Except for very large animals, burial on your property (unwrapped except perhaps for a light cloth) is an option. City ordinances typically require burial of domestic ani-

mals at least 3 feet below the surface. Other op-
tions: Many animal shelters will accept deceased
pets for cremation at no charge, though a donation
will be welcomed. Some communities have a pet
cemetery. Some vets can arrange to send a pet's
body to a rendering plant for disposal. Rendering
transforms the carcass into useful things like soap
and fertilizer.

To quote the folks at Eco-Cycle, in Boulder, Colorado, "While fiber in food is a good thing, food on fiber isn't." Paper fiber, including the corrugated paper pizza box, cannot be recycled if it's contaminated with food.

PIZZA BOXES

Green way to get rid of a pizza box: Tear off and dis-
card portions of the box that have mozzarella,
tomato sauce, and any other stuff stuck on. Place
the clean remainder in your paper recycling con-
tainer. The same goes for all other carry-home boxes
made of paper. Unfortunately, many "doggie bags"
are made of expanded polystyrene, better known as
Styrofoam, which can't be recycled, period.

**PLASTIC WATER
BOTTLES**

True confession: I have drunk from the cool well of bottled water and I'll certainly do so again—without remorse. For reasons that are not completely understood, bottled water has become astoundingly popular. One motive may be nothing more, nothing less than hospitality. Offering a bottle of water is simple kindness; receiving it is simple pleasure. That's a pretty good transaction.

But then there's the other side. The national addiction to bottled water makes no sense when you study the numbers. Ounce per ounce, bottled water costs 10,000 times more than tap water (it really does—run the numbers). And the trash pile of discarded bottles is enormous. The industry says it produced 39 billion water bottles in 2007, or about 130 for each man, woman, and child—are you doing your part? The recycling industry says four out of five bottles were dumped.

Once upon a time, "bottled water" meant the 10-gallon glass bottle inverted at the office water cooler. Out of the office for a jog, you stopped at a drinking fountain that ran continuously—some people called them "bubblers." But drinking fountains are in fixed places, and we're a nation on the move. Bottled water fits our lifestyle.

Green way to behave around your disposable water bottle: Refill the bottle with tap water and reuse it two or three times before you drop it in the recycling bin. Sure, the bottle must remain clean—dump whatever water remains, rinse well, refill, refrigerate. If everyone reused a plastic bottle of water just once, yearly sales of plastic bottles would be cut in half.

Even if it's clean, plastic food wrap goes in the trash. Municipal recycling programs generally are unable to recycle it.

PLASTIC WRAP

This applies to mouse, rat, and roach traps of all kinds. Wear gloves, disposable gloves if possible. Drop the trap into a plastic bag. Tie shut. Drop that bag into another plastic bag and tie shut. Drop in trash can. Dispose of gloves. Wash your hands.

RAT AND ROACH TRAPS

SEPTIC TANK CLEANERS

Septic tank and cesspool degreasers that contain organic solvents such as petroleum distillates (check the label) may dissolve grease but also pass straight through the septic system and into the earth, posing a threat to groundwater. Experts say you can reduce the use of such cleaners by keeping food fat out of the septic system (trash it instead) as much as possible.

Green way to dispose of septic tank cleaners: Put them aside for the next household hazardous waste collection.

SHOE POLISH

Green way to get rid of shoe polish and dye: Open the container and let the contents dry hard. Throw in the trash.

SHOES

This section is about athletic shoes—running shoes and tennis shoes, mainly. Other kinds of shoes are lumped in with "Clothing."

In a college town, a favorite way to dispose of old running shoes is to tie the laces together and hurl the pair onto a utility wire above the street, where they swing in the wind for a season or two. In my town, fifteen pairs swing on one wire at the moment. Score!

Green way to get rid of worn-out athletic shoes: No excuse accepted for tossing them in the trash. Take a look at this website: www.runtheplanet.com/shoes/ selection/recycle.asp. Run the Planet provides all kinds of resources for runners, including places to recycle old shoes. At the website you can find a number of U.S. and foreign listings. Probably the best known is Nike Reuse-A-Shoe—old shoes are ground to crumbs and mixed with binders to produce new running and playing surfaces. For example, resurfacing a running track will use about 75,000 pairs of shoes in a 10% to 20% blend with the binder.

All Nike stores and many other stores accept old shoes—all brands—for recycling. Some community collection programs send old shoes to poor people abroad. For example, First Christian Church of Jacksonville, Florida, sends shoes to Haiti. TeamBarrios LLC, Denver, sends shoes to Mexico.

SIX-PACK YOKES

The plastic punch-out that connects some six-packs of soft drinks, water bottles, and beer cans is a brilliant packaging invention—cheap, strong, sleek, easy to hold. Unfortunately it's also long-lasting. If Jacques Cartier and friends had popped a six-pack on the banks of the St. Lawrence in the year 1534 and left the trash behind ("Mon Dieu!"), the plastic connector would remain more or less intact today. Plastic persists, as we are reminded by six-pack yokes strewn along the roadside and floating in the seas.

Green way to get rid of a plastic drink-bottle yoke: Cut the rings apart and throw in the trash for landfill disposal. Although the plastic is theoretically recyclable, few if any collection programs include yokes in their programs.

SMOKE AND CARBON MONOXIDE DETECTORS

The most common type of smoke detector contains a very small amount of the radioactive substance americium-241. That's why these smoke detectors are labeled for radioactive content. But the Nuclear Regulatory Commission says the amount of americium-241 is so small that smoke detectors present no health threat. It's okay to throw them in the trash. But there's a better alternative . . .

Green way to get rid of a smoke detector: Return it to the manufacturer for recovery and reuse of the americium. You should find the company name molded into the detector or on a label on the back side. Use Google to get a company address. Wrap the detector well, labeling it "For Disposal Only—$0 Value."

Green way to get rid of a carbon monoxide (CO) detector: CO detectors are relatively new on the scene and uncommon in the disposal chain. Before tossing in the trash, turn the CO detector off by pulling out the activation tab below the small marked rectangle on the rear panel. To get at the tab, use a small coin to twist and break the bottom edge of the detector case.

SPRAY CANS

If there's any pressure left in a spray can, it can explode during rough handling in the garbage collection or disposal process, possibly injuring workers. The other problem is what's inside the can—probably a chemical that should be kept away from water sources.

Green way to get rid of spray cans: If the can is empty and contains no pressure, you may be able to include it with other household recyclables—check with the authorities first. If you can't recycle such a can, toss it in the garbage. But if the spray tip is clogged and you cannot relieve any residual pressure or evacuate the contents, set the can aside for delivery to a hazardous waste collection center.

STEEL (TIN) CANS

They're often called "tin" cans but they're actually made of steel, which is "North America's No. 1 recycled material," according to the Steel Recycling Institute. Steel cans such as paint cans, soup cans, pork and bean cans, and condensed milk cans were recovered at a 63.4% rate in 2006—the highest ever—and combined with scrap autos, appliances, and other streams of recycled steel to become the principal feedstock of steel-mill furnaces. That pork and bean can may come back as an I-beam or a refrigerator.

Green way to get rid of a steel can: Toss it in the recycling bin. If collection of recyclables is not available where you live, there's still a possibility your steel cans will be pulled out of the garbage if the waste stream passes through a MRF—a "material recovery facility," or "Merf"—where magnets separate steel from the trash.

SUITCASES

You're tired of pulling that bag off the carousel at baggage claim, but it has many good miles left. What do you do with a suitcase that's worn out its welcome but not its useful life?

Among the nation's frequent travelers, seldom by air, are an estimated half-million children in foster care at any one time. Many kids move to a new foster home every few months, and many have to tote all their worldly goods in a few plastic bags. Your gently used suitcase can add some dignity to a difficult time for a child. To contribute a suitcase, call a local social service agency for suggestions. Or go to www.suitcasesforkids .org.

SWIMMING POOL CHEMICALS

I once saw a demonstration of what can happen when certain pool chemicals are mixed with innocent things like soft drinks, as might occur when they're compacted together in a garbage truck. For a minute or two nothing happened, but then there was an explosive flare of fire and smoke. Don't try to replicate this chemical reaction—take my word for it.

Green way to dispose of swimming pool chemicals: Never in the trash; always in a household hazardous waste collection program.

TELEPHONE BOOKS

Phone books used to be banned from paper recycling because of the binding glue. It held the pages tight but was so tough it clogged the paper recovery machines. That's history—bindings are environmentally friendly today. Virtually every recycling program accepts phone books along with other paper.

*Green way to get rid of a telephone book: Drop
your paper directory into a recycling bin. But to save
paper in the future, see if you can switch to a CD-
ROM for white page and yellow page listings. AT&T
produces a CD-ROM in many parts of the United
States. Call 800-745-8720 for info.*

This section is about the old mercury thermometers you stick in the mouth, or elsewhere, to measure body temperature. And it's about the old mercury-containing thermostats that hang on the wall and regulate the warmth or chill of the house. Things that contain mercury must be handled with care—skin contact with the metal can lead to brain damage.

THERMOMETERS AND THERMOSTATS

It rarely happens, but what if you drop an old glass-stick thermometer with mercury inside and it breaks, spilling the silver metal who knows where? It's important to keep toddlers and pets away as you collect as many droplets as you can. You can use a toothpick or piece of paper to push small droplets together into a larger droplet and nudge it into a small container with a lid. Don't use metal as a pusher—the mercury will cling to it. And don't use a vacuum! A vacuum will atomize the mercury and contaminate the machine.

Green way to dispose of a glass thermometer containing mercury: Take it to the household hazardous waste collection site. If you're dealing with a broken thermometer and a drop of recovered mercury, do the same.

Green way to dispose of an old thermostat containing mercury: Thermostat Recycling Corp. maintains an online directory of heating and air conditioning companies that accept old thermostats for recycling. Here's where to go: www.nema.org/gov /ehs/trc/.

TIRES

The recycling and reuse of automobile tires is a huge success story. That was not always the case. Twenty years ago, states were plagued by huge piles of scrap tires that caught fire with alarming frequency or just lay there, collecting water and breeding mosquitoes. In 1990, an estimated one billion tires were stacked around the landscape, awaiting a good idea, which states began to provide in the form of front-end disposal fees added to the price of new tires. That ensured proper handling of your trade-ins. Today, there are end-use markets for 87% of scrap tires generated annually in the United States, and the billion-tire heap of oldies has been whittled back to well under 200 million, says the Rubber Manufacturers Association. A large proportion of old tires are used as fuel in cement plants, paper mills, and electric power stations—tires produce more heat than coal does, pound for pound.

Green way to get rid of old tires: Leave them in the dealer's custody; they'll be handled properly. If you insist on taking an old tire home (maybe to make a swing in the old oak tree), you'll still have to pay the disposal tax.

TOYS

The trick in disposing of toys is to move them from your household to another household while the toys are still popular and serviceable. That way you both acquire space and perform a social good. The window for launching toys into such an orbit is narrow, however. If you wait too long you may be stuck with boxloads of plastic paraphernalia that no kid is interested in. But stuffed animals always seem to be negotiable.

Green way to get rid of toys: With the consent of the owners, give them to another user to enjoy. Or ship them to Grandma and Grandpa's house for those occasional visits. But take care to pass along safe toys. The big scare about lead paint on kids' toys, and small ingestible things like magnets, has made parents vigilant. Hardware stores sell kits to test for lead, priced as low as $5 to $7. For the latest on problem toys, check with the Consumer Product Safety Commission at www.cpsc.gov/cpscpub/prerel /prerel.html.

**WINDSHIELD-
WASHER FLUID**

Green way to dispose of a surplus: Give it away to another car owner. If you can't give it away, flush the fluid down the toilet. Rinse the empty container and recycle it, or use it to store other liquids on their way to reuse, such as motor oil or solvents left over from cleaning paint brushes.

Wire coat hangers are simply packaging, like the plastic bag that covers laundry and dry cleaning. Yet hangers defy disposal, multiplying on the closet rod until they become a nuisance. At our place, gangs of coat hangers are periodically split up and sent to hang out in remote corners of the household. They are incorrigible and inevitably must be evicted, but not without a fight. They instantly turn an empty wastebasket full to overflowing. They catch other trash and poke the lid off the garbage can. They serve no purpose in a landfill and only melt to slag in an incinerator.

WIRE COAT HANGERS

Green way to get rid of wire coat hangers: Most are in mint condition—take them back to the dry cleaner for reuse. Take back the plastic bag, too.

YARD WASTE

If your home is surrounded by grass, bushes, and trees, and you're responsible for keeping everything looking good, you're managing a heavy load of yard wastes. The town of Camp Hill, Pennsylvania, just across the river from Harrisburg, calculates that each resident there produces about 400 pounds a year of leaves, grass, brush, weeds, and tree limbs. The simple math: A four-member household in Pennsylvania produces about 1,600 pounds per year. Nationally, yard wastes compose about 20% by weight of the trash stream. But the whole idea, of course, is to keep yard wastes out of the trash stream.

Green way to get rid of yard wastes: Make it your goal to dispose of all yard wastes on your own property. My cousin Bruce aims to do that. He uses a mulching lawnmower when he cuts the grass—the blades shred the grass fine and blow it down to the soil. He also uses the mulching mower to pulverize leaves. Some people toss grass and leaves (and weeds and vegetable and flower trimmings, and even kraft paper bags) in a compost pile. If you don't have much room to compost you can use a snap-together composting bin, for sale at a home supply store.

The second best strategy is to use the community yard-waste-composting service—either you rake yard wastes to the curb or bag them in kraft paper sacks for scheduled pickup. The County of Los Angeles Department of Public Works has put together an excellent Internet guidebook on all the major techniques for managing yard wastes. Check smartgardening.com or www.ladpw.org/epd/sg/index.cfm. See also the section "Leaves."

Z: EVERYTHING THAT'S LEFT

You've done your best to reuse and recycle, and still there's a pile of stuff waiting for smart, green disposal. Examples are toothpaste tubes and deodorant sticks, waxed cartons, microwaveable food containers, coffee-bean bags, and much more. The common denominator among leftovers is that they are made of several different materials. Unlike an aluminum can or a corrugated box or a laundry detergent jug—each made of a single material—a composite is an artful blend. For instance, a tube of pastry dough consists of a paper core, foil inner and outer layers, and steel end-caps. An aseptic carton of squash soup is similar in design. In both cases, this is brilliant packaging but a bust so far as recycling is concerned. Trash technology isn't smart enough yet to economically salvage the separate ingredients.

We could wait for technology to catch up to the trashy end of the line. But a better approach is to ask what can be done right now at the front end by the three key players: manufacturers, government, and consumers:

- Manufacturers can practice "source reduction" by engineering products for disassembly and reuse of materials at the end of product life. In packaging, for example, that means designing containers that use as few materials as possible so they can be taken apart and recycled instead of trashed.

- Government can promote better manufacturing design and better recovery of resources by enacting front-end disposal fees as part of the retail price of products. A small front-end disposal tax already works beautifully in the

case of automobile tires. Why not do the same
with consumer electronics?

■   Consumers (that's us, folks—we're two-thirds of
the national economy) can exercise the simple
power of choice to reduce trash. Then use your
imagination as you discover the green way to
get rid of practically everything around the
house.

INDEX

ABOUT THE AUTHOR

Norm Crampton has worked in the waste prevention field for a number of years—as secretary of the Institute for Solid Wastes of the American Public Works Association, member of the Solid Waste Advisory Commission of the City of Chicago, and executive director of the Indiana Institute on Recycling. He's the author of the textbook *Preventing Waste at the Source* and the first popular book on household waste reduction, *Complete Trash: The Best Way to Get Rid of Practically Everything Around the House*.